Introduction

I can honestly say that not a single day goes by without someone or something teaching me a lesson. These learning experiences can be blunt tools with profound messages or as subtle, and fleeting as a summer breeze.

Of course, like many of us, my ego sometimes tends to hide from valuable and often timely life lessons. However, any meaningful lesson that life delivers cannot remain ignored for long.

And so, I find my higher-self offers an unerring knack for exposing my fragile ego for what it is: ridiculous, vain and fearful.

Ultimately, it doesn't matter in what form these life lessons are presented; I am grateful for them – *eventually*. Thus, proving the age-old idiom: *an old dog can be taught new tricks*.

And over the ages, there has been a tradition of women and men undertaking spiritual quests to uncover truths, seek knowledge, and gain insight. Perhaps, even enlightenment.

And if, as is oft quoted, '*Enlightenment is when a wave realises that it is the ocean*,' then this is the core message of this book.

A sense that all of us are trying to understand, as best we can, the human experience and its underlying meaning.

And for me, certainly, in this small volume, it is centred in two things.

First, our ability to love ourselves and others. And second, the need for us all to keep learning the absolute truth about ourselves and the world in which we live. One might imagine a different world if we embraced these two seeds of inner divinity.

A world that sees the human species rise finally to the full height demanded by its intelligence, potential and divine nature.

Within *Ten Villages - One Flower*, the main protagonist is uncompromising in the messages he delivers.

Each message is designed to teach the recipient a higher truth with uncomplicated language.

But then, throughout the ages, all great spiritual women and men speak with plainness and truth. From Stoic to Humanist, the central theme of their hope for human greatness is a canon of love and learning.

I hope you find insights to add to your heart-led musings and meanderings about the greatness within you as you read Ten Villages- One Flower.

Steve

The Dream

Each morning in a distant land, the sun meets the desert and mountain as old friends. And deep within a mountain cave lives a wise and venerable teacher.

The hermit is a man of few words, but those who take his counsel believe his wisdom is ancient and from mystical sources.

One night, in a dream, a voice announces to the teacher, "You must visit the ten villages in your community.

Within each village, the unearthly voice whispered, "Someone needing wisdom will be found."

Later, without fanfare or report, the wise man gathered a few meagre belongings and started his journey towards the first village.

The Goatherd

The following morning, as the sun rose above the horizon and having arrived at the first village, the teacher sat on a stone plinth set against an ancient well.

Along one of the narrow streets leading to the well, a man herding goats was muttering and cursing to himself.

His face contorted in anger and irritation.

"You appear vexed," suggested the teacher.

"I am," said the man. "My neighbour angers me. I hate him and the ground he walks on."

"And yet, the teacher replies, you bring him to work with you."

The Olive Tree

Under the shade of an olive tree, the teacher enjoys some respite from the sun's uncompromising heat.

A woman walking by the tree asks if she can share the tree's shade. The teacher nods and says, "Of course."

The woman's hands agitate a string of well-worn burgundy-coloured beads. Round and round, she recycles the circular beads while staring at the barren, dusty ground.

After a few minutes, she lifts her head and looks at the teacher.

"Sir, every day I worry and fear what the future will bring."

"It is a blessing then that here you sit in the present. In the present, you will lose your fear and find peace."

The Fisherman

Meandering along the shoreline of a green-blue sea, the teacher makes his way to a fishing village.

On the beach, a fisherman, recognising the teacher, approaches him and exclaims, "It is an honour that you choose to visit our village."

Offering a low bow, he adds, "In our humble village, you are our treasured guest!"

"You are very kind," replies the teacher with a smile.

Uninvited, the man begins to walk in tandem with the teacher. After a few moments, the man breaks the silence and asks, "Master, can I ask how I can learn to be more patient?"

Time passes and, believing the teacher has not heard him, he repeats, "Master, how can I be more patient?"

More time passes.

Exasperated, the man exclaims, "Teacher, I have asked you thrice to teach me how to be more patient and still you have said nothing!"

"Even so, the teacher replies, you have yet to thank me."

The Merchantman

Sat on a hilltop overlooking a village famous for its trade in spices and silks, the teacher closes his eyes and meditates.

On the last out-breath of his meditation, the teacher opens his eyes.

Unannounced, a merchantman is sitting in front of him. The merchant's silk clothing is refined and expensive.

"Teacher, I am rich. I own many possessions and have many servants and yet, I feel dissatisfied. What is it that will finally fulfil me and bring me peace?"

"Nothing," declared the teacher.

The Orange Seller

Within the heart of a verdant valley sits a village known for its orchards.

On its outskirts, on the road leading to the village, a woman sells oranges from a wooden stall.

"An orange, please," requests the teacher.

"Of course, sir. Please take one as a gift. All have heard of you and your journey through the villages of our land."

"You are very generous, thank you," said the teacher.

Looking anguished, the woman says, "Sir, I feel so alone."

"You are alone because you say you are alone. Yet, you are part of all you have met and have yet to meet. We are all connected – choose to be so."

The Shepherd

Walking through a narrow-cobbled lane
in a quiet hamlet, a small flock of
bleating sheep surround the teacher
and halt his progress.

The shepherd, agitated and red-faced, urges the sheep forward. "Get on, sheep – get on, you stupid beasts!"

When the shepherd sees the teacher, he comes to a halt.

"Teacher, forgive my ill-mannered flock. My mind was in turmoil, and while distracted, I stupidly left the pen open. As you can see, they all escaped."

"Why are you in turmoil?" quizzed the teacher.

"Yesterday, my best friend of many years cruelly betrayed me."

"Then this is a blessing, not a burden."

"You jest, teacher."

"I do not jest. Now the betrayal is over, how happy you must be that forgiveness can begin."

The Widow

Passing through a village late one evening, the teacher caught sight of a woman sitting on her doorstep.

The woman's arms wrapped tightly around her legs, and the occasional movement of her shoulders testified to her weeping silently.

"You are awake late, sister, and I see you so very sad."

She looks up, the full moon giving her tear-stained face an amber hue.

"I cannot sleep because I mourn for my husband. He died suddenly last year."

"Daughter, grief is the desert, and death is the oasis. You belong in neither. Tether your grief to the past and live your life fully now.

Be happy in the love and memories you shared. It is the shade you both rest under until reunited."

The Unloved

Outside a
village, tired
from walking,
the teacher
rests by a
natural spring.

In a quiet
moment of
contemplation, he watches a woman lead
a donkey to the spring so it might drink.

After the donkey quenches its thirst,
the woman ties him to the tree and walks
to where the teacher sits.

"I do not mean to disturb you, master, but I have a constant worry that makes me sad. My problem is that I cannot find love."

"You seek something you already possess," replies the teacher.

The Weaver

The teacher enters a village known for the fine silk carpets its women weave. Outside the front of each house, on two brightly coloured poles, are awnings protecting the women from the sun.

The women chatter and weave their wondrous patterns into the carpets throughout the day. Every carpet is unique; each knot tied a testimony of centuries of knowledge.

Strolling through the village, the teacher pauses, admiring the handiwork and ingenuity of each weaver.

One woman stops working and looks up to see who is watching her weave.

"Sir, I know of you," whispers the woman. Her voice is as quiet as the silk she weaves.

"I spend hours at the loom, and my mind always turns to one thought. I fear dying."

"Sister, it is not living a full life now, which should cause you to fear. Not death."

The Artisan

On a meandering, dusty byway leading to the next village, the teacher crosses the path of a thin willow of a man. His face is as pitiful and downcast as the package-laden donkey he leads.

He looks up, recognises the wise man, and stops.

"I've heard of you," he announces. You are the hermit who lives in a cave. They say you are wise."

Shrugging his shoulders, "Perhaps," replies the teacher.

"Tell me, wise man, why do I labour to create masterpieces of painted beauty, only for people to insult me with their criticisms and opinions?"

"It is true, the teacher replies, that the first arrow always strikes home.

Thereafter, you decide how many find their target."

The Child

Just before dawn, as the teacher starts his journey home, he reaches a settlement of nomads. They have pitched their tents temporarily in ancient ruins within an oasis.

Resting on a small stone wall, the teacher watches the sun rise steadily in the sky, its rays giving lustre to the brightly coloured canvas of the tents in the camp.

"Not a soul stirs until mid-morning, when a couple of women scurry between tents, casting nervous glances at the wise man as they go.

Perhaps, the teacher thought, *my presence disturbs their normal routine. I should leave.*

The teacher begins to gather his belongings when a child surprises him by walking directly towards where he stands.

Her hand, no bigger than a teapot lid, clamps onto one of his fingers.

"Come sit in the shade near the water.

You can drink some water if you want to."

Intrigued, the teacher follows his little guide, smiling as he does.

Under the shade of a Cedar tree, the teacher props his back against its trunk and looks at the child.

"Where are all the people?" he asks.

"Hiding. Everyone says God walks with you. They are scared."

"But God walks with everyone," replies the teacher, smiling warmly.

"I know," replies the child with a shrug of her shoulders. That's why I'm not scared. You're just an old man."

Chuckling, the teacher replies, "Oh yes, I am old – very old indeed."

The girl reaches into a small pocket on the front of her dress. She retrieves a flower.

The yellow petals of a daisy glimmer gold in the sunlight, and she presents the little flower to the teacher.

"See, I carry the Great Spirit everywhere - every day. I want you to have it."

The girl's emerald green eyes shine with pride - her smile as glorious as her gift of gold.

"I thank you for your beautiful gift. But if I take your flower, you will be without God."

"It's okay; the Great Spirit made plenty of flowers."

"And what am I to do if I have no flower?"

"Well, when I travel across the desert with my family, there are no flowers. That's when I carry a flower inside."

"Inside?" quizzed the teacher.

"The Great Spirit travels with me – everywhere and always – inside my heart.

Anyway, I must go now. My mama will worry where I am. Goodbye, old man."

And like a shooting star journeying
across the darkest night, the girl was
gone. Her fleeting presence leaves the
teacher profoundly star-struck.

He levers himself up from his resting
place, gathers his belongings and
restarts his journey home.

As he walks, the child's words tumble
around his heart and mind, "*The Great
Spirit travels with me – everywhere and
always – inside my heart.*"

Gazing upon the delicate flower cradled
in his palm, a gentle smile graces his lips,
which blooms into laughter.

Gradually, the laughter fades as the words of his dream trickle slowly into his felicity.

Like a ray of sunshine breaking through a stormy cloud, a profound realisation gradually makes itself known to him.

"... someone needing wisdom will be found..."

"It seems wisdom found me," he mutters to himself.

A solitary tear meanders down his cheek and falls to the dusty ground. A happy testimony of life's simplest meaning: that love and learning are everywhere.

THE END
Omnia Vincit Amor